Survivors of the Holocaust

Jane Shuter

www.heinemann.co.uk/library
Visit our website to find out more information about **Heinemann Library** books.

To order:
☎ Phone 44 (0) 1865 888066
🖹 Send a fax to 44 (0) 1865 314091
💻 Visit the Heinemann Bookshop at www.heinemann.co.uk/library to browse our catalogue and order online.

First published in Great Britain by Heinemann Library, Halley Court, Jordan Hill, Oxford OX2 8EJ, part of Harcourt Education.
Heinemann is a registered trademark of Harcourt Education Ltd.

Editorial: Andrew Farrow and Dan Nunn
Design: David Poole and Tinstar Design Limited
    (www.tinstar.co.uk)
Illustrations by Martin Griffin and Nicholas
    Beresford-Davies
Picture Research: Maria Joannou and
    Thelma Gilbert
Production: Viv Hichens

Originated by Ambassador Litho Ltd
Printed in China by Wing King Tong

ISBN 0 431 15373 6
07 06 05 04 03
10 9 8 7 6 5 4 3 2 1

British Library Cataloguing in Publication Data
Shuter, Jane
    Survivors of the Holocaust – (The Holocaust)
    1.Holocaust, Jewish (1939–1945) –
    Juvenile literature
    2. Holocaust survivors – Juvenile literature
    I.Title
    940.5'318

A full catalogue record for this book is available from the British Library.

Acknowledgements
The publishers would like to thank the following for permission to reproduce photographs:

AKG p. **38**; Anne Fox/Vallentine Mitchell pp. **8**, **9**; Art Archive/National Archives p. **6**; Auschwitz-Birkenau State Museum pp. **22**, **25**, **31**, **35**; Eva Panas p. **39**; Houghton Mifflin pp. **12**, **14**, **15**; Rudolf Vrba p. **40**; Emma Robertson/Magnet Harlequin pp. **23**, **30**, **33**; Estate of Hugo Gryn pp. **26**, **27**; Gerda Weissmann Klein pp. **11**, **18**, **21**; Hulton Archive p. **48**; Leiberose Archive p. **28**; Leon Greenman pp. **44**, **45**; Naomi Gryn p. **29**; Popperfoto p. **17**; Rich Cohen p. **16**; USHMM pp. **4**, **10**, **13**, **20**, **24**, **34**, **36**, **37**, **41**, **43**, **46**, **47**, **49**; Weiner Library p. **32**; Yad Vashem p. **42**

Cover photograph reproduced with permission of Hulton Archive.

The Publishers would like to thank Jonathan Gorsky of the Council of Christians and Jews for his assistance in the preparation of this book.

Every effort has been made to contact copyright holders of any material reproduced in this book. Any omissions will be rectified in subsequent printings if notice is given to the publishers.

Contents

Words appearing in the text in bold, **like this**, are explained in the Glossary.

The Nazis and the Holocaust

In 1933 the **Nazi** Party, led by Adolf Hitler, came to power in Germany. It wanted to create a new German empire, the **Third Reich**. This new empire would be far bigger than Germany, so the Nazis began to plan how to take over other countries. They also believed that the Germans were superior to all other races, so they began to discriminate against anyone who did not fit their idea of a 'perfect' German.

Czech political prisoners

When Germany invaded Czechoslovakia in 1939, many Czechs fought back. Those who were caught, like the men in this photo, were sent to the camps.

The camp system

The Nazis arrested anyone they saw as a political opponent and put them in special prison camps. These were different from ordinary prisons because camp prisoners were not given a trial and had no date for their release. They lived and worked in appalling conditions and they died, or were killed, in large numbers. The first of these camps, Dachau, was set up just four days after the Nazis won power in the March 1933 election.

The camps were run by the **SS** (short for *Schutzstaffel* – security staff), which had been set up as Hitler's private bodyguard. They all swore an oath of loyalty to Hitler, not Germany. The SS grew to take over parts of the army and to run the camp system. The camps were very effective. By 1935 very few Germans openly opposed the Nazis. So instead of political opponents, the Nazis filled the camps with people they considered '**undesirable**' – people such as drunks, criminals, the unemployed, Jehovah's Witnesses and those who the Nazis saw as belonging to 'inferior races'. The Nazis had very firm, but very wrong ideas about race. They invented a race, a group of people with the same ancestors far in the past, called **Aryans**. According to the Nazis, these people had pure German blood and were superior to all other people. The Nazis thought that Aryans could take what they wanted and do what they liked to people from other, 'inferior' racial groups.

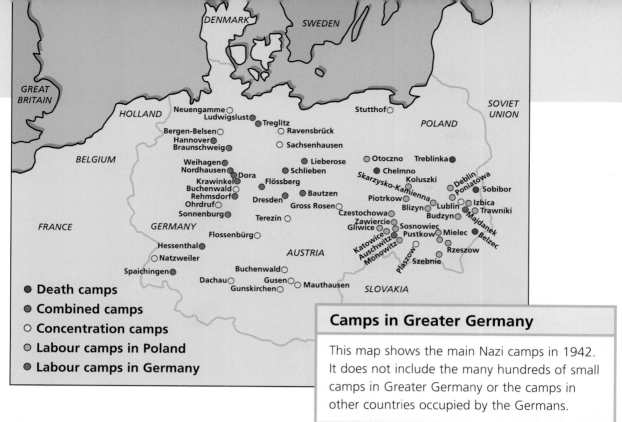

Death camps

Death camps
Combined camps
Concentration camps
Labour camps in Poland
Labour camps in Germany

Camps in Greater Germany

This map shows the main Nazi camps in 1942. It does not include the many hundreds of small camps in Greater Germany or the camps in other countries occupied by the Germans.

The Nazi empire

The Nazis began to build their empire by taking over other countries. In 1938 they took over Austria and part of Czechoslovakia. In 1939 they invaded the rest of Czechoslovakia and, later, Poland. Britain and France eventually reacted to the invasion of Poland by declaring war on Germany on 3 September 1939. But by this point the German army was taking over more and more land. The Nazis made people in all these lands obey Nazi laws. Their opponents in these countries were also put into the camps.

The Holocaust

The camps played a large part in the **Holocaust** – the deliberate attempt by the Nazis to kill all Jewish people in the lands they controlled. The Nazis used the first camps as prison camps for political prisoners. Many of these were Jewish, but they were imprisoned for their political beliefs, not for being Jewish. Many people died from the harsh conditions in these early camps. However, even when the Nazis found that they had broken down most political opposition, they did not close the camps. Instead they expanded the camp system.

As we have seen, the Nazis filled the camps with all those people who did not fit into their Nazi state or who came from racial groups that the Nazis believed were inferior to the Aryan racial group. People belonging to these racial groups, such as gypsies and Jews, were given the worst jobs in the camps and died in their thousands from harsh treatment. But the Nazis decided they were not dying fast enough. They wanted to kill all the Jewish people in the lands they controlled. So they set up special camps, **death camps**, just to murder thousands of Jewish people each day.

Survivors

Millions of people died in the Holocaust – many historians estimate about 5.7 million Jews alone. Very few people sent to the camps survived. Often there was only one member of a large family – although some people were lucky enough to find another close relative who had survived. At first, the survivors were not encouraged to talk about their experiences. No matter where they set up home after the war, people's first reaction was something like: 'It's over now, you were lucky, put it behind you and make a new life.'

As time passed, people were more willing to listen to the survivors' stories, but some found it difficult to believe that they were telling the truth. However, the survivors, many of them young people, had much more complicated reactions. They wanted to forget, but they could not. What had happened was real; they had lived through it; they had lost family and friends to it. They felt lucky to be alive, but they also felt guilty and unworthy. They had been treated like animals for so long that it took them a while to adjust to 'real' life. For them, the camps had been real life – it was the new lives they were just beginning that seemed unreal.

How did they survive?

Most survivors agree that, while there were things that people could do to improve chances of survival, most survived by luck, or the will of God. It helped to have the support of loved ones; it helped to have been young and healthy at the start. It helped to have confidence and a hope of survival. But all of these things did not count at all if people upset an SS guard, or even just ended up in a group controlled by a particularly sadistic guard. Nor did they affect the work people were given, or even the camps individuals were sent to. That was down to luck.

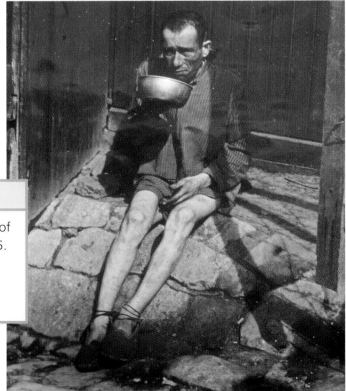

A survivor of Buchenwald

This survivor was photographed after the liberation of Buchenwald camp by the US Army on 11 April 1945. The liberators tried to record as much of what they found as possible because they knew that people would find it hard to believe.

Some survivors' views on how they survived

Primo Levi was an Italian Jew who became a famous writer:

'The ones who adapted to everything survived. Most did not adapt, and died. Shoes, for example. They would throw two deliberately mismatched shoes at you. One with a high heel, one without. We had to make complicated exchanges to find two shoes that fitted. Some feet swelled, rubbed against the shoe and became infected. At the hospital swollen feet were not treated – those who had swollen feet were sent to the gas chambers.'

Tadeusz Sobolewicz was a Polish **partisan** fighter who was sent to Auschwitz:

'The answer is very simple. Any one of those who were killed could have survived. I could have easily been one of those who died. All these factors contributed: strong will, stamina, the length of stay, food, health, the ability to get on with other prisoners, friendship and the help of others. Some were saved by faith in God or by a deep conviction that they would survive.'

Abba Kovner, a Jewish partisan, spoke to survivors just after the end of the war:

'Why do you think you survived? Because you are smarter than those who died? Because you are better? No. You survived for one reason: you were lucky.'

Elie Cohen was a Jewish doctor who was in Westerbork camp in the Netherlands and in Auschwitz:

'Hope was both very important and very unimportant. It could keep you going. Pessimists died fast. But it could not actually save you.'

A former member of the female orchestra at Auschwitz, interviewed anonymously, said:

'Being part of a group was vital. There was a good group spirit in the orchestra and people kept you going when you might have given up had you been alone. We hustled each other to stay alive, to stay on course, to stay disciplined.'

A sense of worth

It was hard for many survivors to get used to not being seen as vermin, which is how the Nazis had treated them. Indeed, in some places, and the survivors mention Poland most often, some people were still influenced by Nazi **propaganda**. They blamed the Jews for the war and treated survivors who tried to return home badly. Some survivors themselves had trouble in seeing themselves as 'real people' at first.

Gerda Weissmann Klein remembers her **liberation**:

'The soldier jumped from the truck and greeted me. I must tell him, I thought, from the start. Remember, for six long years the Nazis had treated us like dirt. "May I see the other ladies?" he asked. He probably doesn't know, I thought. I must tell him. "We are Jews," I said in a small voice. "So am I," he answered.'

Getting out early

The Kindertransports

Some Jewish people decided to leave Germany almost as soon as the **Nazis** took over. Sometimes it was impossible to get a whole family out. Many sent their children to safety. After a wave of Nazi brutality against Jews in 1938, Britain agreed to take 10,000 Jewish children aged three months to seventeen years without visas, just identity cards. The children had to have homes to go to – either families or hostels set up by charity organizations. These rescue trips were known as ***Kindertransports***.

Anne Fox

Anne Fox left Berlin on a Kindertransport in December 1938, aged twelve. Her parents stayed behind in Berlin, because they could not get visas. Anne's brother, Gunter, in England on a student visa, found a Jewish family to take Anne in:

> 'Mrs Pincus was kind, but she was not my mother, nor could her house replace our flat with its central heating and other comforts. At school, there was another German refugee in my class and we were happy to be together, to speak our own language and laugh at the strange ways of the British.'

Evacuated

When war broke out, in September 1939, Anne's school was evacuated to the countryside and she went to live on a farm in Swineshead, a small village near Bedford. The village people were kind and welcoming and all the children were uprooted, so her position was not as odd. On Anne's fourteenth birthday her mother wrote: 'I would have liked to bake a cake for you, but you will have to make do with this picture from a cookbook.' Anne still has the picture. In February 1941 she went to a school run by and for refugees from Hitler's Germany.

Life in Cardiff

When Anne passed her exams at sixteen, she went to Cardiff in Wales, to live with her brother and his wife, Connie. Her first job was with a dressmaker: 'Miss Litchfield was supposed to train me, but left me in a room all day ripping seams and sewing hems.' She only stayed a week. Connie found her a job in the local library.

London, 1938

This photo was taken when Anne arrived in London in December 1938.

The end of the war

When the war ended, Gunter contacted various organizations to try to find their parents. In September 1945, a letter arrived saying that Wilma Oppenheimer, a survivor now living in Denmark, remembered their mother from the camp at Terezín. They wrote to Wilma, who wrote back saying both parents had been in Terezín. Anne's father had died there. Her mother had been sent on a **transport** and had not contacted Wilma after the war. Wilma was sure she was dead. Anne says: 'I did not grieve, I could not grieve. I had been a orphan for six years already and there was no funeral, no grave, no relatives left.'

A new life

Anne went on with life as before. Shortly after the end of the war she met Frank Fox, a Jewish American soldier, at the library. They fell in love and got married in January 1946. Frank was sent home by the army in February and Anne waited for her visa and other documents to arrive. When they came, in May, she went to Southampton: 'The ship waiting to take us to America was the *SS Washington*, the same ship that had brought me to England.' Anne and Frank settled in America and had a family.

Swineshead village school

A photo of the village school taken during the war. Anne is at the back on the far right.

Uncomfortable survivor

Anne survived the **Holocaust**. She says that when she compares her war years with those of survivors trapped in Germany she feels uncomfortable being called a survivor. But she was separated from her parents at twelve, had to cope in a strange country, had to face finding out what had happened to her parents. When she went back to Germany with Frank:

'I scanned the faces of the older people. Where were they when the Jews were being persecuted and gassed?'

She also visited Terezín, where her parents had been prisoners, and Auschwitz, where her mother was killed.

'We, who were spared, must tell our children, so that they can tell their children what took place.'

Fighting back

Not all the Jews who left Germany early were children. Jews of all ages emigrated from 1933 onwards, in increasing numbers. Some were lucky enough to settle far away from the expanding borders of the German **Reich**, in countries that remained free throughout the war – for example, the USA, Britain and Palestine. Some of these people joined the armed forces of the country they were living in. Some returned to Germany to fight. This was even more dangerous for them than it was for the people they fought beside. If they were captured and the Nazis discovered they were Jewish, they were sent to the camps, not treated as prisoners-of-war. Others were smuggled back into **occupied** Germany to work with the **resistance** and **partisan** groups there. Others still, such as scientists and mathematicians, used their special skills against Germany from their new homes.

Kurt Klein

Kurt Klein was born in Walldorf, Germany in 1920. When the Nazis came to power in 1933, Kurt's parents wanted to leave Germany. Like many families, they tried to get visas to emigrate. Kurt's sister left for the USA in 1936 and got a visa for Kurt in 1937. A year later, their brother joined them. Once one family member was in a country it was easier to get another visa. However, it was a race against time to find the money and the various **papers** and visas they needed. During the *Kristallnacht* attacks of 1938, when the Nazis organized attacks on Jews across Germany, Kurt's parents were forced out of their home and their possessions were ransacked. In 1941 they were rounded up and sent to Gurs camp, in France. Their visas came through in 1942, but it was too late. Kurt's parents had been sent to Auschwitz.

Fighting in the US Army

These Jewish soldiers fought in the US army. They were photographed near the US camp at Aachen, Germany, in 1945.

Fighting the Nazis

When the USA joined the war in 1942, Kurt, as an American, was drafted into the army. He spoke good German, so was made an intelligence officer. In 1945 Kurt was a lieutenant with the 5th US Infantry, advancing through Czechoslovakia. His unit was busy liberating camps, rounding up Germans and questioning them. As a German speaker, Kurt was often needed in several interrogations at once. He remembers how the captured soldiers denied supporting the Nazis:

> 'I thought I was fighting the Nazis. Yet I questioned many, many soldiers without finding one willing to admit to being a Nazi.'

It was especially hard for him, as a Jew, to cope with what the Nazis had done to Jewish people. He had set off for Europe with the hope of finding his parents, but as the scale of the Holocaust became clear to him, that hope faded.

Kurt Klein

This photo of Kurt Klein was taken in 1945, the year the war ended.

Building a future

One of the labour camps the 5th US Infantry liberated, in May 1945, was Volary camp, where Kurt met Gerda Weissmann, a prisoner in the camp. She was in hospital for many months. Kurt visited Gerda almost every day and helped her get in touch with her only surviving relative, an uncle in Turkey. They fell in love. When he was sent to Munich in late June, he could no longer visit, but wrote letters to Gerda, who joined him in Munich at the end of July. Kurt was sent home to the USA in September 1945. He proposed to Gerda, but they had to wait to marry until her papers came through in 1946. Kurt ran a printing works in Buffalo, New York. It eventually became clear that Kurt's parents and Gerda's family had not survived. Kurt and Gerda gave talks to various schools and other groups and wrote books on their experiences, feeling that it was their duty, as survivors, to do so.

Going into hiding

People who did not get out of Germany early enough had to think of other ways of surviving. One option was to go into hiding. This was easiest for people who did not 'look Jewish'. **Nazi propaganda** showed Jews as dark, with dark skin and heavy features. It was easier for blonde, blue-eyed Jews with pale skins to pretend to be **Aryans**.

Rosette Goldstein

This photo of Rosette Goldstein was taken during the war. Rosette, on the right, is with Mrs Martin, the farmer's wife, and her youngest daughter. The Martins took a risk in hiding Rosette and probably saved her life. But, despite their kindness, she never felt she fitted in. Many other hidden children felt the same.

Hidden children

It was dangerous for a whole family to go into hiding. Many families split up – some only had the chance to hide one person, usually a child, who was hidden with non-Jewish people. These people took a big risk. Some children spent the whole war with one family. Others were moved around. Some of them were well looked after, while others were treated badly. All of them were scared at the separation. Many of them survived and were the only survivors from their families.

Rosette Goldstein

Rosette Goldstein's parents left Poland for France soon after Hitler came to power. Rosette was born in Paris in 1938. When the German army **occupied** France, the family was in danger again. In 1942 Rosette's father, who was working as a lumberjack, asked a local farmer to hide Rosette.

Into hiding

The farmer agreed, so Rosette's mother put her on the train from Paris:

> 'All of a sudden I was sent to this farm, to live with people I did not know. I remember going on the train with Jean Raffa, a friend of my father who was a Christian. I remember eating hard-boiled eggs and bread and butter and being warned that if anyone asked, I had to say he was my father. I was lucky, because my father was at the farm on the first night, so I felt safer.'

More hidden children

The boys shown in this photo, taken on a French farm during the war, were Jewish children in hiding.

There were good and bad aspects to life on the farm. Rosette remembers:

'We were lucky to always have food, because it was a farm. There were chickens. We made our own butter, even our own soap. There were three girls in the family. I can't say that I suffered, but I was lonely, I had no friends. They were good to me, but sometimes, if she was cross, the youngest, who was fourteen, would say things to me like "You dirty Jew". The girls were so much older than me, they were working on the farm all the time, they had no time for me, or if I got to do anything it was watch the cows all day with the youngest girl.'

Nearly caught

Rosette had to be careful not to be caught, but sometimes curiosity got the better of many of the hidden children:

'One day I saw soldiers with rifles coming to the farm. They had come for food, for the chickens. The farmer's wife put me in the bedroom, under the mattress. I got out and went to look through the keyhole and I could see the Nazis standing in front of the chimney in the next room. I was lucky. They didn't search the place.'

Reunited

Rosette's mother survived the war in Paris, pretending she was not Jewish. She was never caught. When the war ended, she went to find Rosette. They went back to Paris and began rebuilding their lives without Rosette's father, who was killed at Auschwitz. Rosette found it hard to forget the war years, although she knows she was 'lucky':

'Nobody wanted to listen to us. They all said, "You were very lucky, that's it. Don't talk about it anymore." But I knew it made me different. When we hidden children meet, we are drawn together by the fact that we are different from other people. I didn't see myself as a **Holocaust** survivor at first. But that is what I am.'

The ghettos

As the Nazis took over Eastern Europe they set up **ghettos** and herded Jewish people into them. Ghettos were walled or fenced-off areas of a town or city where all Jews had to live. Once the ghettos were set up, Jewish people from Germany were sent there and then Jews from occupied western Europe were crammed in as well. During the Holocaust, Jewish people were taken from the ghettos to the camps.

Zelda Polofsky

Zelda Polofsky was born in about 1932, in a small town near Vilna in Lithuania, part of Poland before the war. The Nazis occupied the village in 1941. Zelda remembers their arrival. The Jews from the village were herded into a town ghetto. Her father and some other men made a hiding place for several families, carefully dug under a building that had no basement, fearing that worse was to come.

A narrow escape

Zelda remembers they only just escaped the massacre in the Vilna ghetto. She had been ill and, waking early and feeling better, went for a walk:

> 'It was only just light. I went down to the lake and saw a policeman with a gun there. He wasn't supposed to be there, so I went and told my mother, "Something doesn't feel right". So we went to the hiding place. As we went we could hear shooting, there were

Happier times

This photo shows Zelda Polofsky, sitting down, and her older sister, Droysk, before the war. Droysk fell sick and died while in hiding.

people running all over. People were running into the water of the lake, dragging their children. We hid for days. The men went out at night. They said all the houses were empty. They took what food they could find for us. The Germans had put out signs saying: "We know you are hiding. Don't be afraid. Come out and you will be safe, we will give you work." But we stayed put.'

They were found after five days in hiding, but were not shot at once. They were imprisoned and Zelda's father managed to bribe a guard to let ten men, women and children leave the ghetto and go into hiding.

Hiding

A local farmer hid the runaways, but there were too many of them for him to hide for long. They moved on to another farm, but could not stay there long, either. There were so many of them, it was hard to stay hidden and people were soon talking about them. They went into hiding in the woods. The farmer brought them food when he could and they begged and stole food from other farmers. Zelda remembers:

> 'They begged from other farmers and at night, they took what they could from the fields – carrots, potatoes. I got sick and whatever food my family had was given to me. My mother gave me all the food; maybe it would have kept her alive. And I took it, never questioning.'

A death

Living in the woods in the rain and snow of winter, with hardly any food or shelter, was desperately hard. Sometimes some of them found shelter in a barn or shed, but seldom for long. The group eventually broke up. Then Zelda's mother became ill:

> 'We were hiding in a haybarn and my father had left to find food. My mother kept calling, calling for him. When he came at last she said, "You're here. Now I can die." And she did.'

After the war

After the war, Zelda and her father spent some time in a **displaced person camp**. This card was given to Zelda when she left, to prove she did not have any infectious diseases.

Liberation

The family stayed in the woods for four years, until the end of the war. Zelda's sister died, but she and her father survived, although they were both sick by the time they were liberated by the Russians. They went home, but found that only 27 of the 550 Jews that had lived in their town had survived. The remaining local people were hostile, blaming all Jews for the war. It was clear that they could not stay there, so they moved on. They eventually settled in the USA.

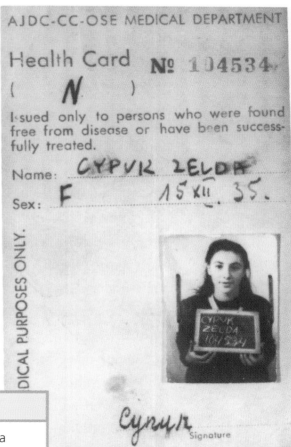

AJDC-CC-OSE MEDICAL DEPARTMENT

Health Card   No 104534.

(N)

Issued only to persons who were found free from disease or have been successfully treated.

Name: CYPUK ZELDA

Sex: F   15 XII. 35.

MEDICAL PURPOSES ONLY.

Cynyk
Signature

Fighting from hiding

Many people who went into hiding had to concentrate simply on staying alive. Some groups of people became **partisans** – they hid in the forests, but fought the Nazis whenever they could. Depending on how they were armed, and where they were hiding, they blew up roads, bridges and railway lines, killed soldiers, stole supplies and smuggled others to safety. Some partisan groups were large and well organized. Some even had contact with the world outside Nazi Europe and were sent weapons, money and other supplies.

Ruzka Korczak

Ruzka Korczak grew up in a Jewish community in Poland. She joined a **Zionist** youth group and was determined to go to live in Palestine. In 1939, when she was eighteen, Hitler invaded Poland. Ruzka made her way 483 kilometres (300 miles), mostly on foot, across Poland to Vilna, where she heard that Zionist youth groups were gathering to go to Palestine. She set up home there with some other Zionists, all about her age. Among these were two people who were to become her lifelong friends: Vitka Kempner and Abba Kovner.

In June 1940 the Russians took Vilna. The Zionist groups broke up. Some were arrested. The rest moved on. Ruzka headed for home, but the roads were blocked. She had to go back to Vilna, which had just been occupied by the Germans. She and Vitka were forced to live in the medieval Vilna ghetto, which had just six streets for 30,000 people. Because they had lived in Vilna for a while they were lucky – they knew someone who took them in. There were ten boys and two girls in just three rooms. Some Zionists joined the ghetto police. This meant that when two of them were on duty together at the gate they could smuggle food and weapons in and out. But it soon became clear that the Germans were moving more and more people out of the ghetto to an uncertain fate. Then news came that these people had been mass murdered in the nearby woods. It was time to act.

Fighting together

This photo of Ruzka, Abba and Vitka was taken in Vilna, shortly after the war ended.

Fighter and carer

Ruzka fought with the partisans in the ghetto and later when they went into hiding in the woods. She was also in charge of their health and the very limited supply of food. When some bread was stolen, the thieves were caught and sentenced to death. Ruzka thought it was harsh, but right: 'It was a powerful lesson. Stealing stopped in the camp.'

The partisans

Abba Kovner, the leader of the group, held a ghetto meeting for the toughest young people his group could find. He told them only 17,000 people remained of the 80,000 Jews that had once been in the ghetto. The rest had been murdered. He urged them to fight. Many agreed, so they began to train them, to get weapons. Guns were smuggled into the ghetto from outside in many different ways, including through the sewers by men posing as workmen laying pipes. The sewers were a good way to move around the city – inside and outside the ghetto. Ruzka found a book, in Finnish, in the ghetto library. It described all sorts of methods of **guerrilla fighting**, including how to make cheap bombs. They began to follow the instructions. Ruzka also spent a lot of time walking the streets, trying to convince young people to join the resisters. Groups of partisans slipped out from the ghetto and blew up railway lines and caused other disruption.

Living in Israel

This photo, taken in 1948, shows three survivors from Buchenwald farming fruit on a kibbutz near Jerusalem.

They began leaving the ghetto in small groups, to set up home in the forest. Once enough of them were out, the others, including Ruzka, tried to start a ghetto rising. It failed because most people would not fight. The partisans left the ghetto and continued to fight from the Rudniki forest, about 19 kilometres (12 miles) away from Vilna.

They were there for two years. It was hard, especially as they had decided to stay a Jewish group, rather than join other partisan groups in the forest. The peasants would help other groups, but refused to help the Jews. Ruzka took part in many dangerous partisan actions, blowing up bridges, railways and weapons trains. In 1944 the group destroyed 51 trains, hundreds of trucks and dozens of bridges. After liberation, Ruzka finally got her wish and went to live in Palestine, as did Abba and Vitka.

Surviving the camps

From 1938 onwards, Jewish people were sent to the camps for no other crime than being Jewish. It was not until 1941 that the **Nazis** set up **death camps** to do nothing but kill Jewish people as efficiently as possible. However, by that time, thousands of Jews had already died due to the horrific conditions in the camps, where they received the worst treatment of all the Nazis' prisoners.

Gerda Weissmann

Gerda Weissmann was born in Bielsko, Poland, on 8 May 1924. She was fifteen when the German army **occupied** Poland, in September 1939. Her father was ill when the German army marched in. The family had been warned of the danger. A telegram came from Gerda's uncle Leo in Turkey saying: 'Poland's last hour has come. Dangerous for Jews to remain. Visas waiting for you in Warsaw embassy. Come at once.'

Gerda's mother decided they had to wait until her father was better. The German occupation was completed with stunning speed. By 4 September the streets were full of soldiers and many local people were greeting them with cheers. Nazi swastikas appeared everywhere. That evening a neighbour called: 'She told us that during the afternoon several Jews had been rounded up and locked in the synagogue, which was then set on fire. "Men had better stay out of sight," she whispered.'

Trapped

It was dangerous to go out, dangerous even to answer the door: 'We heard of German soldiers coming to a house for information and if a man answered the door they took him away; often that was the last the family saw of him.' It was difficult to decide if it was safer to stay or to go. Some relatives who tried to escape had their train bombed, were rounded up by the army and only just escaped being shot. They returned to hide with the Weissmanns. On 17 October letters came ordering all men between the ages of 16 and 50 to register to work for the Nazis. Gerda's brother Arthur and his cousin David went to register. The next day, Arthur left. He asked them not to go with him to the station. It was months before they heard from him again. Then they heard that he and David had escaped and were in hiding.

Before the war

This photo shows Gerda Weissmann at fifteen. It was taken in 1939, the same year that Germany invaded Poland.

Moving around

This map shows Bielsko and the camps that Gerda worked in during the war.

GERMANY

POLAND

Berlin

Grunberg

Christianstadt

Marzdorf   Bolkenhain

Helmbrechts   Landshut

Cracow

Prague   Bielsko

CZECHOSLOVAKIA

AUSTRIA

● Camps that Gerda was imprisoned in

Changes in Bielsko

Bielsko was close enough to the German border to be sucked into Greater Germany. This meant that the Nazis were committed to making it *Judenfrei* – 'Jew free':

> 'Late in November a letter came saying all Jews had to report on Monday, 2 December 1939 to a building in Herman Goering Strasse. We had to leave out valuables and the keys for the house, clearly labelled, in the front hall of the house.'

The Weissmanns sold what they could, but did not get much money for it. The next day, news came that the deportation had been postponed. But government actions against Jews became stricter:

> 'After Christmas our rations were cut to less than half the rations of non-Jews. In the New Year we were ordered to wear white armbands with a blue star and the word JEW on them. Shortly after, this was changed to a yellow star.'

Many Jewish people left Bielsko, but the Weissmanns stayed. On 19 April 1942, the remaining 250 Jews in the town, mostly the old and the sick, were ordered to move to a small **ghetto** set up in the poorest part of the town, just a few houses around a cobbled courtyard. In June the ghetto was broken up, to make Bielsko *Judenfrei*.

Leaving Bielsko

The Weissmanns were told that Gerda's father was to go to one labour camp, Gerda and her mother to another:

> 'We were assembled in a field in Bielsko. After about four hours the **SS** men finally came in a shiny black car, with their shiny boots. They checked lists. We were all there. Why did we all walk meek like sheep to the slaughterhouse? Why did we not fight back, run, hide? Because we did not think that human beings were able to commit the crimes that were being committed.'

They were divided up at the station. Gerda was put in a different group from her mother:

> 'I knew Mama was marching on – in the other direction. I did not turn around. I knew that if I did so we would run to each other and they would beat us, or shoot us. We had to go on alone.'

She never saw her mother again. She was not entirely alone. A friend from Bielsko, Ilse, was with her.

Sosnowitz and Bolkenhain

Gerda's train took them to Sosnowitz ghetto. The girls were taken to a barracks until they were sent off as slave labour to a factory that asked the SS for workers. Gerda and Ilse were chosen to work in Bolkenhain weaving mill and were taken there on 2 July 1942. The director of the factory made a speech: 'We would be taught to weave. If we behaved and worked hard, all would be well; if not, we would be sent back.'

The Jewish woman put in charge also made a speech:

> 'Frau Berger said, "How we feel is beside the point; we have to please the people here. I will personally punish anyone who breaks the rules. One person can make it hard for all of us." She had made it clear where we stood. She had also made it clear to the director that we were not fools. I liked her for that.'

The barracks at Bolkenhain were new, so everything was fresh and clean. It was turning out to be one of the better camps:

> 'We were given warm soup in new bowls and hunks of good bread. After supper, we were allowed to wash, although the water was cold. After that, we were free to sleep.'

Weaving workshops

This weaving workshop was at Novaky labour camp. Many of the smaller camps for women made them work at spinning or weaving cloth.

Working at Bolkenhain

Gerda's day began at 5.30 a.m. and lasted until late in the evening. The girls were first taught to use the weaving looms and then moved on to work in the factory.

> 'We were very tense and frightened because we had been told that each mistake could be counted as an act of sabotage. We worked hard. At first we tended one loom, then two, then three and finally four. It was exhausting. You had to run from loom to loom, eyes straining to follow the movement of the machine. The noise of the looms was deafening.'

The girls did not have to work on Sundays and they were allowed to send and be sent letters. These conditions were better than conditions in **concentration camps** or death camps, but they were still hard and the threat of being sent somewhere else was always there.

Moved on

In August 1943, the mill at Bolkenhain was closed. The war was going badly and there was not enough yarn for the machines. The girls were divided into groups. Gerda and Ilse managed to stay together and were taken to Marzdorf:

'We were met by our new camp commander, a girl of about eighteen, tall and blonde. Whip in hand, she was shouting at the Jewish woman in charge of the workers. It was very different. My heart sank.'

Marzdorf was an older, more disorganized camp. The work was far harder, including stacking big bundles of flax: 'Our arms became bloody, swollen and infected. The thick dust irritated eyes and wounds and made it hard to breathe.'

As well as her mill job, Gerda had to work much of the night shovelling coal. Luckily she and Ilse were among a group sent to Landeshut camp, to work on weaving looms again. Here they only worked one shift, the night shift, from 6 p.m. to 7 a.m. with a break in the middle for a bowl of soup. They were not allowed mail, but had Sunday off. Many of the girls were now friends and could help each other keep going. Even so, the work was hard and rations had been cut even more. Then, on 6 May 1944, the girls were told that they were going to a larger camp. This was Grunberg. The girls working in the spinning room there regularly became ill and were sent to Auschwitz to be gassed.

Death march and liberation

Gerda and her friends were put on the death march from Grunberg to Helmbrechts. There were 2000 in Gerda's group. Only 120 lived through it. Gerda was one of them. Ilse was not.

By the time they were **liberated** Gerda says: 'My mind was so dull, my nerves were so worn out with waiting, that I just sat and waited for whatever would happen next.'

What happened next was that they were liberated by American soldiers. One of these was Kurt Klein (see pages 10–11), who visited Gerda in hospital. They fell in love, married and went to live in Buffalo, USA. They wrote several books about their **Holocaust** experiences and set up the Klein Foundation, which works to teach young people 'tolerance for differences in others'

The Kleins today

For many years, Gerda and Kurt gave talks about their wartime experiences. They felt that people needed to remember the Holocaust and learn tolerance for one another.

Political prisoners

Jewish people suffered the worst treatment and conditions in the camps. But there were other groups, too, that the Nazis saw as coming from inferior racial groups and who were also treated especially harshly. Two such groups were Russians and Poles, whom the Nazis saw as belonging to a race they labelled 'Slavs'.

Tadeusz Sobolewicz

Tadeusz Sobolewicz was only seventeen years old when he was arrested in 1941 as a '**political**'. He and his family had been involved in the Polish **resistance** movement and he had been on the run for some time. He was imprisoned, questioned and sent to Auschwitz I. Tadeusz remembers arriving in Auschwitz with a trainload of other politicals:

'The platform was full of SS guards. Each had a submachine gun or rifle. Some had dogs. Our guard opened the doors and undid the barbed wire [the prisoners had been bound together with this wire]. We tumbled out to shouted orders and suddenly, for no reason, the SS began hitting people. We were marched to the camp, where we were handed over to prisoners in striped uniforms, each armed with a pole or club, who marched us to "Reception".'

At the 'Reception' building the prisoners went through the usual processing:

'We were ordered to undress and put our belongings into paper bags. We

Happier times

This photo shows Tadeusz Sobolewicz in his boy scout uniform. It was taken in 1935, when he was eleven years old.

handed these to prisoner **functionaries**, gave them our details and were given a prisoner number. This number and our names were written on the bags, which they took away. Next, they shaved our heads. After that we had to walk, naked, to the bathhouse. I had not washed properly in months, so stepped eagerly into the shower. The water was almost boiling. "Too hot for you? I'll make it cooler," shouted the inmate at the controls. He made it freezing cold. We then had to line up, still naked, cold and dripping water, for underwear, uniforms and wooden clogs. It took hours until I was finally handed the red triangular badge with my number, 23053. We were sorted into block groups and marched to those blocks. Standing outside, we were given needles and thread to sew our badges on. We had had nothing to eat all day.'

Auschwitz

Tadeusz was in Block 9, with a few other people he knew from the resistance movement. Their block warden made them take off their shoes and herded them into a bare room. They were given a blanket each, but slept on the floor: 'The five of us lay down together in the first space we could find. We were all cramped up like sardines in a tin.'

A man, clearly unwell, who couldn't make it out of the room to the toilet in time, was beaten to death in the corridor. Tadeusz could not understand the continual shouting and brutality. One of the older men said: 'Wise up, Tadio! They don't need a reason to beat us, they'll do it for nothing. Try not to put a foot wrong.'

The prisoners were woken early, with more shouting. They had to put their clothes on, hand in their blankets and go to the washroom to splash water over their faces and hands:

> 'We had to line up in the corridor. At the end of the corridor, a ***kapo*** was ladling a sort of hot grey liquid into tins. Once this was drunk it was roll call in front of the block. We were lined up and taught what to do. It takes time to teach 400 prisoners how to take off their caps and put them back on at exactly the same time. Many newcomers did not speak German (orders were always given in German) and had no military training.'

The main gates

This photo shows the main gates of Auschwitz I. The words over the gate say 'Work will set you free' in German.

The rest of the block groups were sent off to work. The prisoners from Block 9 were newcomers and had not yet been sorted into work groups. Block 9 had to work on following orders all together. They practised roll call drill and also hopping like frogs. They were beaten over and over; several were beaten to death. Priests and Jews were hauled out of the line and either beaten to death or marched away for 'special treatment'. Then the group was marched off to be photographed, something that should have been done the day before, but the SS had run out of film.

Work

At about noon on the first day, Tadeusz and the other prisoners were given more 'soup'. They were then marched off to the yards by the station where the building materials were stored:

'Each of us had to take two bricks and return to the column, holding them level with our heads. We then had to run back to the main entrance, piling the bricks where the new blocks were being built. We then had to reassemble, run back and go through the whole process again, but faster. If prisoners lost their grip on the bricks and dropped them this was 'sabotage' and earned them a beating. We had to pass those who lay on the ground and keep going.

Exhausting work

Prisoners in all the camps had to do exhausting, often pointless, work all day. These prisoners are in Buchenwald camp.

Soon those of us left standing were out of breath, sweating, exhausted.'

This went on all afternoon. On the last return to the camp the prisoners had to carry seven dead bodies, as well as the bricks. Work was followed by evening roll call. By the steps of the block lay the day's dead – they had to be counted, too. There were ten dead in all on the first day. After roll call, the prisoners were given a piece of bread and a spoonful of beetroot jam. Then it was bedtime:

'Before we could collect our blankets and lie down, the block warden inspected our clothes, to make sure the triangles were properly sewn on. Again, there were several beatings. "We have to be so careful!" I thought. I was terrified and exhausted by the work, lack of food and a whole day of trying not to get beaten up. I couldn't even cry.'

Tadeusz's life in Auschwitz and the other camps he was later moved to varied in many ways. He was given different work to do, all of it hard, some of it almost impossible. He was sometimes so ill he had to be taken to hospital; he was always sick in some minor way because of the appalling living conditions. But in one important way, every day he spent in the camps was the same as the first – the casual brutality, the beatings, the fear, were always there.

Physical scars

This photo of Tadeusz Sobolewicz was taken in 1945. It shows scars from his ill-treatment in the camps.

Liberation

Tadeusz was moved from Auschwitz to other camps: Buchenwald, Leipzig, Mulsen, Flossenbürg and Regensburg. In April 1945, he and about 1000 other Regensburg prisoners set off on a death march deeper into Germany:

'The SS surrounded the column; the march was very fast. After two hours, prisoners began falling behind. They were shot. I was at the front, pulling a food wagon. We managed to slow the column down, so that more people could keep up.'

By the fourth day they had run out of food. There were far fewer prisoners – almost a third had died of exhaustion, been shot by the SS or managed to slip away and hide. That night, several of the SS slipped away, too. But the remaining SS kept the column marching and kept shooting the stragglers. By the fifth day, there were just 300 prisoners left. When they stopped at dawn an SS officer came to the barn and said Hitler was dead and the SS officer in charge of the column had fled. In the morning, news came that the Americans were about 10 kilometres away. Tadeusz and his friends decided to hide in the barn and risk being found and shot on the spot. The villagers hid them until the American army arrived.

Going home

Tadeusz and his friends were told that they should report to a **DP** camp:

'"Oh No!" No more camps, we decided. The American told us that we should at least go to one for long enough to have medical check-ups, but he would find us a place to stay outside the camp. He did. Next day, when I was examined, I was found to have TB. It was many months, in 1946, before I could go back to Poland.'

When he got back he found that his mother, who had been sent to Ravensbrück camp, had survived. His father had been gassed at Auschwitz. His younger brother had survived the war as part of a **partisan** group. When Auschwitz was set up as a museum, Tadeusz worked there, helping to make sure that the Holocaust was not forgotten. He still lives in Poland.

Hugo Gryn

Hugo Gryn was thirteen in April 1944, when the Nazis took over his hometown, Berehovo, in Czechoslovakia. Berehovo had been under Hungarian control since November 1938. The Hungarians were allies of the Nazis at this time. Because of this, Hungarian was the official language and laws had been passed against Jewish people. But somehow people managed to carry on with their lives. The arrival of the Nazis increased the persecution at once. The soldiers marched in, took hostages and demanded huge ransoms. The Nazis also set up ghettos. Hugo Gryn's memories here come from a statement he gave to officials in Budapest in July 1945, after he had returned home.

The ghetto

Hugo remembers: 'Part of Berehovo was cordoned off on 20 April 1944 and defined as a ghetto. Six thousand Jews came to the ghetto from the town alone, and as many from the surrounding areas. So the total number of Jews in the ghetto came to twelve thousand people.' Now the Jewish people in the area had been cut off from everyone else. Like all ghettos, Berehovo ghetto was badly crowded. People were uprooted from their homes and crammed in with what few possessions they had been allowed to take.

Before the war

This photo, taken before the war, shows Hugo, his parents and his younger brother, Gabi.

The journey

The ghetto was only intended to be a temporary stopping point. By this time, the Nazis had already decided on their 'Final Solution' to what they called 'the Jewish Problem'. This solution was mass murder, so trains soon began running to what was, at first, an unknown destination – the death camps. Hugo's family were deported along with everyone else:

> 'On the 28th May the deportations happened. I was put in a wagon along with the remaining Jews and my family – my parents and a younger brother. After a journey of three days, during which we suffered badly from thirst, we entered Auschwitz.'

Berehovo's children

Gabi's class in Berehovo's Jewish Elementary School, photographed in 1942–3. Every single child in this photo was gassed at Auschwitz.

Auschwitz-Birkenau

The three-day journey to Auschwitz in crowded wagons was exhausting. When they arrived at Auschwitz-Birkenau, Hugo and his family were herded off the train with everyone else and their bags were taken. They then had to go through 'selection' and this is when the family was broken up: 'After arriving in Auschwitz we were divided up. I remained together with my father. My mother and my brother were snatched from us ...'

Hugo's brother, Gabi, was sent to the gas chambers of Auschwitz-Birkenau, something he and his father had explained to them by other prisoners as the usual outcome for those not chosen to work. Hugo's mother was lucky not to be sent there, too. Shortly after their arrival at the camp, Hugo and his father heard that she had been sent to a women's labour camp.

Leaving Auschwitz

Those who were chosen to work at Auschwitz-Birkenau did not spend long in the camp. There was no work in Auschwitz-Birkenau itself because it was a death camp. People there were simply waiting for their turn in the gas chambers. From time to time, a transport of workers was collected up and Hugo's father decided that, no matter what skills were required, they should lie to get on to the next transport out. When the call came, it was for skilled building workers and they stepped forward. They were chosen to go on the work transport. Hugo remembers: 'Father and I remained only a week in Auschwitz, then we went in a work gang, which was intended for work in Lieberose, between Cottbus and Guben. The convoy consisted of 2400 men, all Hungarian Jews.'

Lieberose

Lieberose was a small camp, in the middle of woodland. It turned out to be one of the better camps. The workers there were being used to build a holiday town for German officers at Ullersdorf. They built the houses and drains and ran in the electricity supplies. While conditions here were better than in many camps, they were still bad, as Hugo recalls:

'In Lieberose, we were used for building work, and barracks and houses made of stone were built. The work itself might have been OK, because each person was employed accorded to their strengths. And we were housed in half-human quarters, so that we could sleep properly. But the treatment we had was unbearable. Punishments and other hard mistreatments were the order of the day, without us being even slightly at fault. As for the rest, we were worked almost to the death, with food so bad that we mostly left it.'

Marching west through Germany

On 2 February 1945 Lieberose was evacuated ahead of the advancing Soviet army. Hugo and his father were well enough to take part in the death march, as they were healthier than many in the camp:

'Now it was really clear what the health situation of the camp inmates was. Out of the 2400 that came here [in Hugo's transport from Auschwitz], there were only 150 in a fit state to walk. The rest of them had to be left in the care of the hospital. After we left, the hospital was set on fire, and the people in the hospital all died.'

The prisoners (about 1400 in all) had to walk to Sachsenhausen, which they reached on 10 February. Five hundred of them died on the eight-day journey, which covered over 160 kilometres (100 miles). They only stayed in Sachsenhausen for three weeks and then were marched on again, this time to Mauthausen.

Lieberose

Prisoners from Lieberose camp in Upper Silesia, Germany, pictured connecting electricity to the Ullersdorf holiday town site.

Going back

Hugo Gryn, photographed when he returned to Auschwitz in 1989.

This meant that, by each morning, the weakest that night had been crushed to death. It was also full of contagious diseases. On 4 May 1945 the US 71st Division liberated Gunskirchen. The soldiers moved everybody to a clean German army barracks near by, at Horsching. Hugo and his father had survived. But unfortunately the death marches had badly weakened Hugo's father:

> 'My father, who was then forty-five, had already found himself in a severely weakened condition by the time he came to Mauthausen, because of the unbearable hardships, the marching and the lack of food. Here he got very sick and died in hospital on the 16th May.'

Hugo spent six weeks at Horsching, recovering his strength and trying to come to terms with the death of his father, a death made worse by the fact that it happened so soon after their liberation. He was still not yet fifteen years old. Hugo hoped that his mother would be alive, so went back to Berehovo and she was there. While she was not yet ready to leave, she encouraged Hugo to leave Berehovo to carry on his education. He went to Prague, then Britain, and then moved to the USA to study as a **rabbi**. Hugo married and had four children. He eventually settled in London and became famous as a broadcaster, as well as a rabbi. He died of cancer in 1996.

Mauthausen

By this time, most of the camps in the west of German-controlled territory were in uproar, as they were crammed full of prisoners marched from camps in the east. Some camps were shooting new arrivals on the spot, others put them into tents outside the camp, guarded by the soldiers who had marched them there. Mauthausen was, luckily for Hugo, one of these camps: 'In Mauthausen we were kept in quarantine and stayed there for six weeks. Outside the concentration camp, a tented camp was set up, which housed the Hungarian workers.'

Gunskirchen and liberation

After six weeks the Hungarian workers were marched off again, this time to Gunskirchen. They arrived there on 16th April. Gunskirchen was badly overcrowded, so badly that each night 2500 prisoners were being shoved into huts that were supposed to hold 300.

Lucie Adelsberger

Lucie Adelsberger was living in Berlin and working as a doctor when the Nazis came to power. As a woman and a Jew, Lucie was someone the Nazis did not want working in the Nazi state. She was not allowed to work in the health service, and then she was not allowed to treat **Aryans** at all. Lucie's mother could not get a visa to leave Germany. Lucie remembers:

> 'I loved my mother very much. When she fell sick I refused my last chance to emigrate. She had had a heart attack and needed care all the time. A nurse looked after her in the day and I cared for her at night. Should I let her be deported? I as a doctor, could prevent it. I could save her by killing her, painlessly. I couldn't do it.'

Deportations

Deportations out of Berlin began. Lucie remembers:

> 'How can anyone imagine what it's like to tremble at the arrival of the mail (three deliveries a day), expecting to be called to the **Gestapo**, or told by the **Judenrat** to evacuate on a certain date – you and your husband, or parents, or son, or anyone else you love. You learn to fear the doorbell, too, especially late at night.'

On 6 May 1943 she was arrested. On 17 May she was put on a transport to Auschwitz: 'not from one of the main train stations, but from a small station on the outskirts of the north of Berlin, mostly surrounded by warehouses. The Gestapo liked to keep what it was doing quiet.'

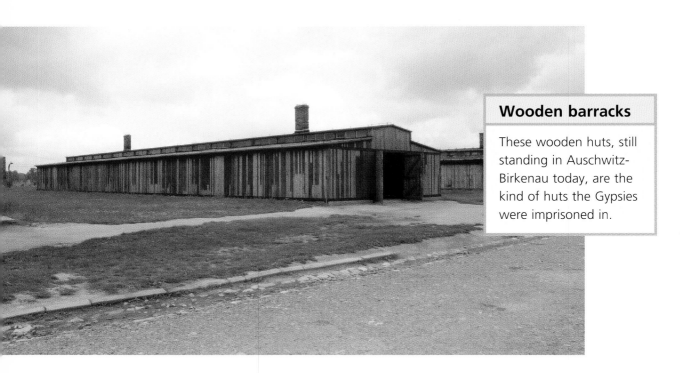

Wooden barracks

These wooden huts, still standing in Auschwitz-Birkenau today, are the kind of huts the Gypsies were imprisoned in.

After liberation

This photo shows the inside of a hut of the kind the Gypsies were crammed into. The picture is from a Soviet film of the camp, made just after liberation.

Arrival

The train arrived at Auschwitz-Birkenau two days later. Lucie remembers being marched to Auschwitz-Birkenau with about 260 other prisoners. They were stripped of all they had managed to keep hold of in the unloading process, then shaved, showered and given uniforms. Lucie and two other doctors were taken to the area of the camp where, for some reason, the Germans kept the Gypsies altogether. All other groups were separated by age and sex. Various diseases had broken out in this part of the camp.

Working in the hospital

The three doctors began work in the 'hospital' at 4 a.m. the next morning. They joined a group of several so-called doctors and nurses, most of whom had no qualifications. Like all the other barracks in this part of the camp, a wooden stable designed to hold 54 horses was now holding 800 to 1000 people:

'The doctors had hundreds of patients to care for. They had to fill out detailed notes for each of them every three days. They also had to keep a completely accurate count of their patients. There wasn't much time for treatment. There wasn't much medicine, either. The only thing we had in any quantity were sacks of a white powder called *bolus alba*. We gave it as pills for stomach upsets, sprinkled it on wounds and rashes and even mixed it up in a paste and painted the bunks and walls with it. All we could really do for the patients was to comfort and encourage them. It didn't make them any better; they still died like flies.'

On the night of 31 July 1944, the SS killed all the Gypsies. Lucie was moved to the women's camp. On 18 January 1945, Lucie's part of the camp set off on a death march to Loslau, where they were crammed into open coal trucks and taken to Ravensbrück. Here the group was broken up and moved to smaller camps. They expected liberation at any time. It took until 2 May for the Americans to reach the camp Lucie was in. Lucie went to live in the USA, where she continued to work, as she had before the war, researching allergies and infectious diseases. She died in 1971.

Surviving by co-operating

Prisoners had a better chance of survival in the camps if they had an 'easy' job. These jobs always had a price attached. Sometimes it was that you were in charge of other prisoners and had to be brutal to them to keep your job. Other prisoners worked in the offices, keeping the **Nazi** system going, while the worst job of all was clearing out the gas chambers in the **death camps**.

Fania Fenelon

Before the war Fania Fenelon, who was half Jewish, was a singer, living in Paris. During the war she carried on singing and worked for the French **resistance**. She was arrested in 1943 and sent to Drancy camp. From there she was moved to Auschwitz-Birkenau on 20 January 1944. On the train she made friends with a woman called Clara, sharing her black market food with her. Fania remembers arriving at Auschwitz:

'We had been travelling for over fifty hours. The smell was dreadful. At first, supervised by the **SS**, the men in each carriage had emptied the toilet buckets, but that didn't last. Our bucket had emptied itself by overturning. We were desperately thirsty. The air was stinking and no fresh air was coming in. We were suffocating. Our door was opened; everyone rushed to it. We were told to get out, to leave the luggage. SS soldiers climbed in and threw out the ill, the slow and the corpses. Living skeletons in striped uniforms, their skulls shaven, moved among us, took the luggage, carried it away. Trucks drove up, with red crosses in white circles on them. "The Red Cross is here," said Clara. "We're not in any danger."'

Chosen to live

Fania and Clara were not loaded on to the vehicles, which were not actually Red Cross trucks – they took people to the gas chambers of Birkenau to be killed. Fifty men and fifty women were chosen to live from that transport of about 1200. They were marched through the snow for half an hour until they arrived at Auschwitz-Birkenau: 'We were herded towards a brick building marked "Reception Block".'

Drancy

Fania spent nine months in Drancy camp in France, before she was sent to Auschwitz-Birkenau.

Uniforms

This photo shows some uniforms now on display at Auschwitz. By January 1944, there were so many prisoners that the camp was running out of uniforms. Clothes stored from earlier arrivals were used, often with a broad blue stripe painted onto them, until enough people died for there to be spare uniforms again.

A vital conversation

Fania had only been in Auschwitz for a day before she had an unexpected opportunity of a better chance of survival:

> 'In the middle of the babel a Polish woman was shrieking for *Madam Butterfly*. "What's she saying?" I asked.
>
> "She's looking for musicians, for the orchestra." An orchestra here? I must have misunderstood.
>
> "What did you say?" I insisted.
>
> "The orchestra, let it drop. What does it matter to you?"
>
> "But I can play the piano and sing Madame Butterfly."
>
> "Well, go and tell her."
>
> I leant over, tried to attract her attention. She didn't see me. I was forbidden to get down, but I did. In a fog, aching all over, I hobbled over to the huge **kapo**. She stared at me suspiciously. I was so small, so dirty, spattered with mud and blood.
>
> "Follow me."'

First days at Auschwitz

At the 'Reception Block', Polish girls filled out forms about the prisoners. They were stripped and then shaved. Fania remembers:

> 'Tattooing came next. I watched as the number 744826 appeared on my forearm. By now I had understood. I was no longer anything, not even a slave.'

They were kept waiting in a large building for some hours and then ordered out:

> 'My bare feet were awkward in the men's shoes I had been given, one yellow shoe and one black boot, about size ten, when I took a size four. How could I march in line or keep in step with these on my feet?'

Fania and the others were taken to one of the brick barrack blocks. Fania asked the block warden what had happened to the people in the trucks. She did not reply at first. Then Fania was dragged to the door: 'She pointed to a smoking chimney: "You see that smoke, over there? That's your friends, cooking." "All of them?" "All of them."'

Chosen for the orchestra

Fania was taken to a large, warm, well-lit room. She was told to play the piano and sing. She was told she could join the orchestra. Taking a huge risk, she demanded that they take Clara, too. They did, because Clara could sing beautifully. Clara and Fania were given clothes that fitted. Fania was even given a pair of fur-lined boots. Their barrack was clean and they had a bed each, with a sheet and a blanket. They were allowed to shower every day. But they were not safe. As Fania was told when she arrived: 'We were set up on a whim and we could vanish on one, too.'

Pleasing the SS

The girls who had been in the orchestra for a while told Fania that the SS wanted to hear famous music, even though there were not enough girls to play and some of them did not play very well.

Fania took on the job of rewriting the music the SS wanted to hear so that the girls could play it:

'We did seventeen hours of music a day. Then there were the concerts for the SS, whenever they called for them, to relax after their 'hard' work. It was pleasing the SS at these concerts that kept us alive.'

The orchestra had to keep playing, to do their best, even in the most awful circumstances. At one concert, Fania remembers:

'I saw one woman run up to the electric fence and grip the metal. Her body twisted violently, shaken by the current. A friend rushed forward to pull her off and was also fixed to the wire by the current. No one moved. The music played on; the SS listened and talked among themselves.'

Camp orchestra

This photo shows the men's orchestra at Auschwitz I. Several other camps also had orchestras.

Last days

As the **Allies** advanced, rumours floated round Auschwitz that the Nazis were losing. Fania noticed: 'Our SS seemed uneasy, their morale was crumbling.'

But they did not slow down the killing. Instead they worked faster, running the **crematoria** day and night – 24,000 bodies a day. The orchestra was broken up. Fania and some others were marched to Bergen-Belsen, which was full. They were put into leaky tents nearby. Fania caught typhus and nearly died, as did many of the others. The SS were told to burn and destroy the camp on 15 April 1945: 'We were to be shot at 3 p.m. The British arrived at 11 a.m.'

Liberation

When the British arrived, Fania was very ill, but knowing they had been liberated gave her hope. Her friends asked her to sing. She did so:

'I straightened up and sang the *Marseillaise* (the French national anthem). A Belgian officer handed me the most wonderful present: an old lipstick. I couldn't think of anything lovelier, despite it being three-quarters used by a total stranger. The person with the microphone said: "Please, Miss, it's for the BBC." I sang *God Save the King* (the British national anthem), then the *Internationale* (the Russian national anthem). The Russian prisoners joined in. I sang and from all the corners of the camp dying skeletons stirred, got up, grew taller. A great "Hurrah" burst out – they had become men and women again.'

Remembering

Fania survived and so did some other members of the orchestra. In her book about her experiences, *Playing For Time*, she says: 'I think I've achieved more or less what I wanted for myself now. I wanted to sing, and I've done that now for 25 years.'

This does not mean that Auschwitz is forgotten: 'Particularly at night I find myself back in the block at Birkenau. I spend every night there – every night! I've never left the camp, not for thirty years.'

Elie Cohen

Elie Cohen was a doctor in Aduard, a village near Groningen in the Netherlands, when war broke out in 1939. He was 30 years old. In May 1940 the German army took over the Netherlands. On 8 February 1941, Elie and his wife and baby son moved to Groningen and lived there in hiding. They planned to escape to Sweden, but were caught by the **Gestapo**. They were arrested.

Separated

A relative persuaded the Gestapo to give him the Cohen's baby, now two years old. Elie's wife was put in prison. Elie was sent to Amersfoort **labour camp**. Luckily a nurse in the women's camp knew him: 'She got me a job looking after US prisoners in a nearby camp. I was given more food. I was not beaten any more and this saved me.'

On 8 December 1942, Elie was moved to Westerbork camp. The SS decided to keep him on as a doctor, rather than send him straight to the camps in the east.

Collaborating

Elie's wife was allowed to join him at Westerbork: 'We shared a small flat with a German Jewish couple. I had a red stamp on my identity card that said I was not to be transported to Auschwitz.'

Elie bought his safety at a price:

> 'I became the transport doctor. I had to examine Jews selected for **transports** to the east. I could say a person was unfit for transport. If I did this, he and his family were spared. I faked high temperatures and so on to save people.'

But Dr Spanier, the senior camp doctor, found out what Elie was doing and warned him that if he carried on, it would be his family that was transported:

> 'So I knuckled under. I collaborated. It is a terrible word, but I cannot escape it although my situation was impossible. We did the Germans' jobs for them. I don't know if I would have done it if I had known what would happen to them. We were told they were going to work camps.'

Westerbork transport

These people leaving Westerbork camp have been passed as fit to travel by a camp doctor.

Carl Clauberg

This photo, taken by the SS, shows SS doctor Carl Clauberg and his staff. They are in the operating theatre in Block 10 of Auschwitz, where he carried out hundreds of experiments on Jewish prisoners.

The wrong choice

On 9 April 1943, the Nazis began to hunt harder outside the camps for Jews. Elie decided their son would be safer in Westerbork, protected by Elie's job. Shortly after this, his wife was accused of saying anti-German things and their protected status was taken away. Two weeks later the family was sent to Auschwitz:

'The selection was made as soon as we arrived. We didn't know what it meant. I waved goodbye to my wife, son and mother-in-law. A couple of hours later a Dutch Jew came up and congratulated me. I asked him why. "Because you are in a work camp and the others are dead," he said. The strange thing is I believed it at once – I accepted it. And I wanted to survive.' Elie managed to get work as a doctor in the medical blocks at Auschwitz.

Collaborating again

Elie found he had to do awful things to keep his job, to survive:

'I had to help the SS doctor, Klein, in his selections. He chose those among the Jewish patients who he thought were no longer worth treating. I had to produce their medical cards and tell him my opinion of their condition. It was useless to pretend, because he could see the state they were in, but we played out the little scene, over and over. And I took part, because I wanted to live.'

After the war

Elie made his way back to the Netherlands, where he settled in Arnhem. He married again and had two children. He wrote a book called *Human Behaviour in the Concentration Camp* and worked as a psychiatrist, specializing in helping survivors to deal with their feelings.

Surviving by escaping

There were people who were swept up in the **Holocaust**, but managed to escape. Men, women and children escaped from **ghettos**, from **transports**, even from **camps**. Depending on their age, sex and appearance they hid in different ways. Some spent all their time hiding. Others managed to join **partisan** or **resistance** groups to fight back.

Ruth Cyrus

Ruth Cyrus was 29 when Germany invaded Poland. She and her husband, George, who was also Jewish, were both lawyers. Ruth was pregnant. As soon as the Germans invaded, George was called into the Polish army and Ruth did not see him again until the end of the war. Once the Germans took Warsaw, Ruth could no longer work as a lawyer. Her daughter, Eva, was born on 4 March 1940.

In the ghetto

In October the Warsaw ghetto was set up, surrounded by high brick walls with splinters of glass and barbed wire on top. In July 1942, the Germans began to transport large numbers of Jews out of the ghetto for '**resettlement**'. A couple of months later, a young man appeared and told us the resettlement trains were going to Treblinka, where people were gassed to death. He had managed to escape hidden under piles of clothes being taken back to the ghetto. Ruth made a decision: 'I would not let myself be taken to Treblinka. I would not let them gas me. When they caught me I would make my escape.'

Ruth got hold of a thin hacksaw blade and practised with the blade for hours on end: 'From the moment I had the blade and had learned to make use of it I felt somehow quieter and I knew they would not get me alive to Treblinka.'

The German invasion

This photo shows German troops occupying Warsaw in October 1939. The Germans completed their occupation of Poland with blistering speed.

Transported

Ruth and Eva managed not to be selected during several German round-ups. Partly this was because Ruth worked for a large factory in the ghetto, but it was also due to luck and quick thinking. But eventually their turn came. They were taken down to the station and shoved into cattle cars. Ruth saw that their cattle car had a high, barred window. Ruth asked two young men to hold her up to saw through the bars. Sawing through bars in a moving train was very difficult: 'My fingers started bleeding, my hand became weak but I kept on sawing.' The blood dripping from Ruth's fingers made the bars slippery and harder to work.

The jump

At last, after several hours, the job was done. Ruth knew she could not throw Eva out of the window – she would resist. Ruth decided she would have to go first, so someone had to throw Eva. Ruth promised all her food to anyone who would help. Two boys agreed:

> '"I'd like to jump first", said one of the boys who had lent me his shoulders. He put his hands against the window frame and jumped. The wind swept him off and that was all.'

Before the war

This photograph of Ruth Cyrus was taken in Warsaw before the German invasion.

Now it was Ruth's turn. She had to ignore Eva's screams:

> '"Mummy, mummy, please don't jump." I plugged my ears. For a moment I concentrated on the technique of the jump itself and, standing on the second boy's shoulders, I grabbed the frame and thrust myself out legs first. I heard the whistle of the wind as I was whirled away. I lost consciousness.'

What happened next?

Ruth woke to find she had been robbed, but the robbers had left her coat, her boots and her hacksaw blade. After a frantic search she found Eva. They were still in Poland. She spent the rest of the war as a 'submarine', pretending she was not Jewish. She found someone to take Eva into their family and after the war she and Eva and George finally got in touch using the various organizations set up after the war to reunite families. They settled in South Africa.

Escape from a camp

The **Nazi** camps were heavily guarded, day and night, to prevent escape. Despite this, people did escape, although many were caught again. The people who had the best chance of staying free were those who made contact with local resistance groups, or those who spoke the same language as the local people, so they could ask for help in a familiar language.

Vrba and Wetzler

Rudolf Vrba and Alfred Wetzler escaped from Auschwitz-Birkenau camp in April 1944. They had been brought to Auschwitz-Birkenau in 1942, from Slovakia. Rudolf, aged seventeen, first worked sorting the luggage of the arrivals at Auschwitz-Birkenau. He was amazed by 'Canada', the huge complex of sheds where possessions were sorted and stored:

'It was an incredible sight, a huge rectangular yard, fenced and guarded. There were several huge storerooms and mountains of trunks, cases, rucksacks and kitbags. I didn't think then where their owners might be – every step brought some new shock.'

Rudolf later worked as a clerk, registering new arrivals. When Rudolf found out that the killings were going to increase, he decided to escape.

He wanted to tell the world what was going on: 'The SS were talking about "Hungarian salami" and "a million units"; it was clear what was going to happen.'

Rudolf hoped the outside world would force the Nazis to stop the killing: 'Panic and active resistance by a million people would have caused havoc in Hungary. That would be better than panic by the burning pits of Birkenau.'

He and a friend, Alfred Wetzler, planned their escape carefully. The SS were extending the camp and work parties were moving building materials around and digging trenches and pits in an area called 'Mexico'. Rudolf and Alfred decided to sneak into 'Mexico' and make themselves a hiding place in a trench just deep enough for two, covered in a heap of wooden planks stored for use. They hid ordinary clothes, some food, water and money in the trench.

Rudolf Vrba

This photo shows Rudolf Vrba's 1946 Czechoslovakian identity card.

The Auschwitz report

The Auschwitz report, and several documents summarizing it, were translated and sent to all the Allied leaders.

Free!

On 7 April 1944, Rudolf and Alfred slipped into 'Mexico' and hid in their trench. They were helped by friends in the camp resistance, who piled wood over them and sprinkled petrol and tobacco around the pile. These strong smells stopped the search dogs smelling the hidden prisoners. They knew they would be missed at **roll call** and that there would be guards and dogs out searching for them. So, they did not try to get away at once. They stayed in the trench for three days. Finally they climbed out at night and made their way south, away from Auschwitz. They had memorized lists of where people had come from, their numbers and names. With the help of local people along the way, they made it to Slovakia, mostly on foot. They got in touch with a Jewish doctor who had not been deported because the SS needed doctors desperately:

> 'I walked into Dr Pollack's surgery, pretending to be a patient. I explained who I was and where I was from. When he heard that all his "resettled" relatives were dead, he became very shaky. He asked how he could help. I told him we had to get in touch with the Jewish Council in Bratislava.'

Pollack put Rudolf and Alfred in touch with the Jewish Council in Zilina. They

EXECUTIVE OFFICE OF THE PRESIDENT

★ WAR REFUGEE BOARD

WASHINGTON. D. C.

GERMAN EXTERMINATION CAMPS — AUSCHWITZ AND BIRKENAU

It is a fact beyond denial that the Germans have deliberately and systematically murdered millions of innocent civilians — Jews and Christians alike — all over Europe. This campaign of terror and brutality, which is unprecedented in all history and which even now continues unabated, is part of the German plan to subjugate the free peoples of the world.

So revolting and diabolical are the German atrocities that the minds of civilized people find it difficult to believe that they have actually taken place. But the governments of the United States and of other countries have evidence which clearly substantiates the facts.

The War Refugee Board is engaged in a desperate effort to save as many as possible of Hitler's intended victims. To facilitate its work the Board has representatives in key spots in Europe. These representatives have tested contacts throughout Europe and keep the Board fully advised concerning the German campaign of extermination and torture.

Recently the Board received from a representative close to the scene two eye-witness accounts of events which occurred in notorious extermination camps established by the Germans. The first report is based upon the experiences of two young Slovakian Jews who escaped in April, 1944 after spending two years in the Nazi concentration camps at Auschwitz and Birkenau in southwestern Poland. The second report is made by a non-Jewish Polish major, the only survivor of one group imprisoned at Auschwitz.

wrote a long report about Auschwitz-Birkenau. Shortly after this, two more Auschwitz escapees arrived in Zilina. They confirmed Rudolf and Alfred's report and said the murder of Hungarian Jews had begun. The Jewish Council combined these two reports and smuggled it out of German-controlled Slovakia to Switzerland. From here it was sent to London and Washington. These governments were slow to act, but did eventually put pressure on the Hungarian government to stop the deportation of Jews. Rudolf and Alfred joined the Slovakian partisans and fought for the rest of the war. Rudolf went to Israel after the war, then moved on to Britain. He finally settled in Canada, working at the University of Vancouver. Alfred stayed in Bratislava, working as a newspaper editor.

Different chances

Jewish people in different parts of Europe had very different chances of survival. People in Denmark worked hard to protect the Jews living there – and many of them escaped the **Nazis**. On the other hand, people in the east, especially those in the path of the *Einsatzgruppen*, were much less likely to survive the Nazi takeover. The *Einsatzgruppen* marched into towns and villages, rounded up all the Jewish people, made some of them dig a huge pit near by and then shot them all. People were also affected by luck – good and bad. We are going to look at what happened to the Jewish people of Eishyshok in Lithuania, between Germany and Russia, and to Leon Greenman, an Englishman living in the Netherlands, whose family had appallingly bad luck.

The Jews of Eishyshok

Eishyshok was a shtetl – a market town where most people were Jewish. As the German army marched east, Lithuania was in a direct line between Germany and the Soviet Union. On 23 June 1941, the German army reached Eishyshok. The **Gestapo** moved in, bringing with them an increasing number of anti-Jewish laws and ever more ways to humiliate people.

On 21 September, the leader of *Einsatzkommando 3* arrived with a large number of armed Lithuanians. Some people began to slip away. Others stayed. Families split up, hoping that at least some would survive. The people of Eishyshok were locked up in the old synagogue for three days without food, water or the use of a toilet. They were then taken to the Horse Market, a large open space where horses were sold. The *Einsatzkommando 3* lists say that on 27 September 1941 they killed 3446 Jews – 989 men, 1636 women and 821 children. In fact, by 27 September all the Jews of Eishyshok were gone. About 5000 were killed by *Einsatzkommando 3*. The men were killed on 25 September, the women and children on 26 September. They were killed in the Old Cemetery, where deep trenches had been dug to keep the cattle out. These became ready-made graves.

Einsatzgruppen shooting

This photo shows an *Einsatzgruppen* shooting in September 1941 in Dubossary in modern Moldova. The soldiers killed 2000 Jews that day.

Zvi Michaelowski

Zvi Michaelowski was sixteen when the Germans invaded Lithuania. He escaped from Eishyshok with his sister when the *Einsatzgruppen* arrived, but came back for more of his family. He was caught. He was in one of the last groups of men taken to the Old Cemetery on 25 September. When they arrived they saw the trenches full of dead people. They were lined up along the edge of the trench. Just before the squad began to shoot, Zvi's father shoved him into the grave. Zvi was soon covered in bodies. He lay there for a long time:

> 'It got darker and darker. It was wet, hot and stifling. There were the sounds of those not quite dead moaning and the odd shot. Then it went quiet.'

Zvi pushed his way out of the heaps of bodies and crawled out of the grave.

In hiding

The Jews who escaped from Eishyshok fled to the nearby forests. During the war, the forests of Eastern Europe were full of groups of people, many of them Jewish, but also Poles and Russians. Some hid in small groups of three or four; others set up family camps. Others still set up **partisan** groups to fight the Germans. Zvi fought with the partisans during the war. He was one of just 114 Jewish people from Eishyshok to survive the massacre and the war years hiding in the forest.

After the war, Zvi was arrested by the Russians. He was sentenced to six years in Siberia, but managed to escape on his way there. He found friends who gave him false papers and he made his way into Poland. Zvi ended up in a **DP** camp called Bad Reichenhall, near Munich. He got married there and he and his wife tried to get to Palestine. The first ship they went on, the *Exodus*, was forced to turn back, but they finally made it there in 1947.

Leon Greenman

Leon Greenman was born in London in 1910. In 1935 he married Else Van Dam, and they moved to Rotterdam to care for Else's Dutch grandmother. By the time their son Barney was born, on 17 March 1940, war had broken out. Both Leon and Else were British citizens, so Barney was British, too. While registering Barney's birth at the British embassy, Leon arranged to leave for Britain with the embassy workers. But events moved too fast. On 14 May the German army began to bomb Rotterdam. The bombing totally destroyed the centre of the city, killing almost a thousand people and leaving about 78,000 people homeless. The embassy people moved out at once and the Greenman family was stranded.

Nazi rule

The Nazis took over the Netherlands with incredible speed and began passing laws against Jewish people. Leon could no longer trade with non-Jews. Making money was not the only problem. Leon remembers: 'Our circle of friends was getting smaller and smaller. Every day we heard of people being taken out of their homes and never being seen again.'

Leon accepted the offer of the Van Nautas, non-Jewish friends of friends, to look after the Greenmans' valuables. He gave them the family savings, his most valuable books and pictures and their British passports: 'I did not trust the Nazis. I thought that, if I were arrested, they would take the passports away and we would have no proof of our British nationality.'

When Leon went back to collect the passports he found the Van Nautas had burned them, because they were scared the Nazis would find out they were helping Jews. So the Greenman family had no passports. The British embassy people had left, so the Swiss were dealing with all British citizens. Leon wrote and visited the Swiss embassy over and over, begging for **papers** to prove the family were British. The papers still had not come when the Greenmans were arrested in the middle of the night and sent to Westerbork camp.

Leon, Else and Barney

This photo of Leon, Else and Barney was taken in 1942, just a few months before they were arrested by the Nazis.

ENQUIRER
DEMANDEUR

Stamp of issuing Red Cross:

Name/Nom .... Mr. GREENMAN,
First Names/Prénoms .... Leo
Date of Birth/Date de naissance .... Place of Birth/Lieu de Naissance ....
Nationality/Nationalité .... British
Address/Adresse .... Hertford British Hospital, Paris, - via BRC, Paris.
Original Home Address (in the case of a Displaced Person)/Domicile dans son propre pays :

Relationship of Enquirer to Addressee/Degré de parenté du demandeur avec personne recherchée
.... Brother
The enquirer desires news of the Addressee and asks that the following message should be transmitted to him :
Le demandeur voudrait des nouvelles de la personne recherchée et désirerait lui transmettre le message suivant:
.... Liberated from Buchenwald, - recovering in British Hospital,
Paris. Want news from you all, hope you are well.
No news of wife and son, deported in 1943.

Date .... 17 May, 1945.

ADDRESSEE
DESTINATAIRE

Name/Nom .... Miss GREENMAN,
First Names/Prénoms .... Kitty
Date of Birth/Date de naissance .... Place of Birth/Lieu de Naissance ....
Nationality/Nationalité .... British

Single — married — widow(er) — divorced (Delete all irrelevant matter.)
Célibataire — marié(e) — veuf(ve) — divorcé(e) (Barrer les mots qui ne servent pas.)
Profession/Profession ....
Last known address/Dernière adresse connue ....
.... 97 Jubilee Street,
London, E.1.

The Addressee's reply to be written overleaf (not more than 25 words).
La réponse du destinataire (25 mots au maximum) peut être écrite au verso.

S & D Ltd.—21817

P.R.59/1937

A hopeful message

Leon Greenman sent this telegram to his sister Kitty in England from the hospital in Paris. At this point he was still hoping that Else and Barney were still alive.

Westerbork

In October 1942 the Greenman family arrived at the nearest station to Westerbork camp in the pouring rain:

'We had to walk the three miles there. It was muddy and walking was difficult. Else carried Barney and a bundle. I carried several bundles, with blankets draped around me. They fell off into the mud over and over.'

At Westerbork the family was separated. Leon asked the chief administrator, Kurt Schlesinger, to put them in the care of the Red Cross as British citizens. They waited, visiting the office each day, increasingly worried because: 'Once or twice a week, to make room for the new arrivals, about 1000 Jews were sent to Auschwitz.'

People did not know what went on in Auschwitz, but they did not want to go. One of Leon's friends in Westerbork, Michael Borstrock, escaped deportation by complaining of severe stomach pains. He was operated on for an ulcer. When the wound was almost healed he was called again: 'Michael tore open his stomach wound to go to hospital again.'

Auschwitz and after

In mid-January 1943 the family were deported to Auschwitz. Leon later heard that a letter saying the family were British and should not be deported arrived the morning that their train left. 'We had been told we were being sent to Poland to work for the Germans. We thought we might be separated, but be able to see each other at weekends.'

They were separated on the platform of Auschwitz-Birkenau. Leon saw Else and Barney loaded into a lorry: 'Else had made two red velvet capes for herself and Barney from curtains, and I could see the hoods. I did not know it was the last I would ever see of them.'

It was. Else and Barney were driven off to the gas chambers. Leon had been selected for work. He survived life in Auschwitz, where he spent much of his time working in the Monowitz factory. He also survived a **death march** from Auschwitz to Buchenwald, where he was **liberated** by the Americans on 11 April 1945. He discovered that only two people from his **transport** to Auschwitz – himself and Leon Borstrock, Michael's brother – had survived. He returned to the Netherlands to find his father was still alive, but he decided to settle in England, where he lives now.

Feelings about survival

We have seen that survivors of the **Holocaust** had very different experiences. However, all survivors shared one experience. They survived. They had spent their time in hiding, or in the **camps**, or fighting the **Nazis**, waiting and hoping to survive. Many were too ill, at first, to realize that the war was over, that they had survived. But eventually that fact became clear to them. Over the next few pages we will see how some of the survivors reacted to the fact that they survived.

Feeling angry

You would expect the survivors to feel angry with the Nazis, with the local people who had not helped them, with anyone and everyone that they could blame for what had happened to them. In fact, many survivors did not feel angry at all.

Elie Wiesel, who wrote about his camp experiences in a book called *Night*, remembers:

> 'Our first act as free men was to throw ourselves on the food. We thought only of that. Not of revenge, not of our families. Nothing but bread. And even when we were no longer hungry, there was still no thought of revenge.'

Harry Spiro, just seventeen when the war ended, remembers being **liberated** in Terezín: 'The Russian soldiers gave us twenty-four hours to do whatever we wanted, even kill the Germans. I don't think any of us did that, I'm not sure why.' A few days after he had been liberated, Jack Rubinfeld, just sixteen, was searching for food near the **labour camp** where he had been a prisoner. He found two loaves of bread:

> 'A German woman with two small children asked for food, saying they had not eaten for a day. I looked around, ashamed to let my friends see. I broke off half a loaf and gave it to them.'

Free at last

This photo shows prisoners in Buchenwald in the days after liberation. Elie Wiesel is in the second row of sleeping shelves from the bottom, second section from the left, by the far post.

How the helpers felt

Some of those who had helped many people survive as part of an escape route were, quite simply, relieved. One escape route member, interviewed in the 1980s, said:

'I wept with joy. At last I could put down the heavy weight I had been carrying for years. I had needed to help, but I knew it put me in great danger. So, I'm sorry to say that my first reaction was as much happiness for myself as for all those Jewish people who were now safe.'

Other people, like Irene Gut Opdyke, had helped fewer people, but these people had become friends. She found them in Cracow after the war: 'I felt like a mother hen who finally has her chicks together again.'

Oskar Schindler also kept in touch with 'his' Jews after the war. The photo shows Schindler in the 1950s with some of the people he saved.

Feeling lost

Many survivors had spent years in the camps, being told they were worthless, being treated appallingly, being told what to do every minute of the day. Harry Green remembers:

'It took a long time to get used to being individuals again. I began to discover that I was a person in my own right – quite a revelation after years of **propaganda** about "vermin" and "parasites".'

Primo Levi, an Italian Jew who later wrote extensively about the Holocaust, remembers the first day of freedom:

'For the whole day we had been too busy to remark on the event which we still felt marked the crucial point of our entire existence. Perhaps, unconsciously, we had looked for things to do to avoid spare time, because, face to face with liberty, we felt ourselves lost, emptied, frozen, unable to play our part.'

Having forced himself to survive, having forced himself to stay fit, Levi now fell sick: 'It seemed as if weariness and illness, like ferocious and cowardly beasts, had waited in ambush for the moment when I dismantled my defences, in order to attack me from behind.'

Talking it through

Some survivors wanted to talk about their experiences, like this survivor photographed with a US soldier after liberation. The photo was posed, but there were many cases of soldiers who became friends with the people they liberated. They visited and listened and often tried to help people to work out what to do once they left hospital.

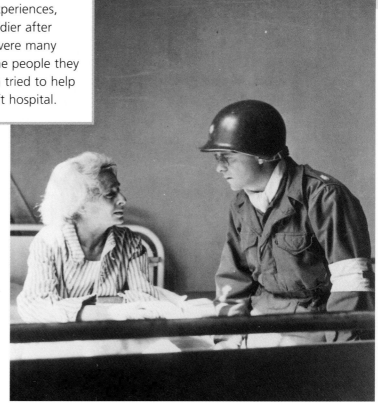

Feeling alone

Many survivors had longed to go home, but not all rushed off when they were liberated. Fania Fenelon remembers:

'Waiting to be repatriated, which naturally required paperwork, we stayed in the camp. It didn't worry us. Oddly enough, we were no longer in such a rush to get back. Normal life worried us; we no longer had the words or the gestures for it. Worse still, who would be waiting for us at the station? Were those for whom we had kept ourselves alive still living? We were still ill, still weak. Life worried us, because we were afraid.'

Edith Kramer-Freund was a German Jew whose husband had died before the war and who spent the war in Terezín. She was sent to Switzerland as part of a group rescued by the Red Cross before the end of the war. She remembers the shock that she and her fellow passengers got when they reached freedom:

'It was a shock to find that we would not, from now on, get preferential treatment. We had held on until liberation. Now we had to fend for ourselves in war-time conditions.'

Feeling threatened

Many survivors who wanted to go home found that they could not. The Nazi Holocaust had been stopped, but there were still Polish and Russian **anti-semitic** groups hunting down and killing Jews. Harry Balsam, Chaim Ajzen, Ben Helfgott and Roman Halter were all boys aged about sixteen who had been liberated from Terezín. They all tried to make their way home, to various parts of Poland. All had to turn back because of threats or stories of Polish groups killing any Jews they could find. They found it incredible that this could be happening after the Holocaust. They joined a group of children nicknamed 'the Boys' who went to live in England. Eastern Europe no longer felt safe.

Feeling guilty

Many survivors felt guilty that they survived when so many millions did not. This feeling was worst among people who had collaborated to survive, such as Elie Cohen (see pages 36–37). But even Jews who left Germany before Hitler came to power, like Frederick Kramer who went to live in Australia in 1932, say they feel guilty, because they think: 'if my life had taken a slightly different turn, it could have been me, I could have ended up in the camps, I could have died. Why have *I* survived when so many died?'

Simon Wiesenthal was a prisoner in the camps. After the war he helped people to trace their relatives and then became famous for his work in tracking down Nazis. He thinks that all survivors feel guilt:

'No matter how hard you try, no matter how hard you bury the camp experience under a successful later life, that feeling grips you, even if you know that you did not harm anyone else in order to survive.'

Needing to remember

Many survivors talk to schoolchildren and students. Some conduct tours of the camps they were imprisoned in. They do this because they feel strongly that young people must be taught about the camps, must be told about those who did not survive by those who did, who were there, whose experiences cannot be denied. Primo Levi explains:

'For the survivors, remembering is a duty. They do not want to forget and, above all, they do not want the world to forget. They understand that their experiences were not meaningless, that the camps were not an accident, an unforeseeable historical happening. In every part of the world, wherever you begin by denying basic liberties, by denying equality, you move towards the camp system and it is a road on which it is difficult to halt.'

Timeline

1933

30 January	The **Nazi** Party comes to power in Germany. Adolf Hitler, its leader, is elected Chancellor.
27 February	Fire breaks out at the Reichstag, the German Parliament
28 February	German President Hindenburg's decree 'For the Protection of the People and the State', allows for the creation of **concentration camps**. The Nazis persuaded Hindenburg to pass the decree to fight what they called the 'Communist threat' after the fire at the Reichstag.
17 March	**SS** set up, formed as Hitler's bodyguard within the army
21 March	Dachau, the first Nazi concentration camp, set up. Concentration camps and **labour camps** set up steadily after this.
26 April	**Gestapo** (Nazi secret police force) formed
14 July	Political parties other than the Nazi Party banned in Germany

1934

20 July	SS now in charge of their own affairs – they are no longer part of the army
2 August	Hitler makes himself *Führer*, sole leader of Germany

1935

15 September	Nuremberg Laws passed against German Jews

1937

16 July	Buchenwald concentration camp set up

1938

13 March	The German army marches into Austria and the Austrian people vote to become part of Germany again
8 August	Mauthausen concentration camp set up
28 October	First Jews deported from Poland by the Polish government
9 November	*Kristallnacht*: Nazi-led violence against Jewish people: synagogues burned, shops and homes looted

1939

1 September	Germany invades Poland. Nazis begin to pass laws against Polish Jews restricting the work they can do, as in Germany in 1933–6. Soviet Union invades Poland from the east on 17 September.
3 September	Britain and France declare war on Germany
28 September	Germany and the Soviet Union split Poland up between them

1940

12 February	First Jews forcibly removed from their homes in Germany and taken to **ghettos** in Poland
9 April	Germany invades Denmark and Norway
27 April	Himmler told to build a camp at Auschwitz
30 April	A large ghetto is set up in the Polish city of Lodz. More ghettos are planned.
10 May	Germany invades Belgium, France, Luxembourg and the Netherlands
22 June	France signs armistice with Germany

1941

6 April	Germany invades Yugoslavia and Greece
22 June	Germany invades the Soviet Union; mass executions of Jews as the German army moves through the Soviet Union
1 September	All German Jews over the age of six have to wear a yellow Star of David with '*Jude*' in black on it
From September	Mass gassings at Auschwitz begin with Soviet prisoners-of-war and continue. They focus on Jews and become more regular from January 1942.
16 October	Mass deportation of German Jews to Poland begins
28 October	10,000 Jews selected and killed at the Kovno ghetto, Poland
7 December	Japan bombs the US fleet at Pearl Harbor, bringing the USA into the war
8 December	First gassing of Jews, at Chelmno
11 December	Germany and Italy declare war on USA

1942

20 January	Wannsee Conference of leading Nazis outlines the 'Final Solution' to what the Nazis call the 'Jewish Problem'
1 March	First deportation of Jews to Sobibor **death camp**
17 March	First deportation of Jews to Belzec death camp
26 March	First deportations to Auschwitz-Birkenau and to the Majdanek death camp
27 March	First deportation of French Jews to Auschwitz
15 July	First deportation of Dutch Jews to Auschwitz
22 July	Daily deportations to Treblinka from the Warsaw ghetto begin
4 October	Himmler orders that all Jews in concentration camps are to be sent to Auschwitz-Birkenau to be killed

1943

19 April	The Warsaw ghetto revolt begins
11 June	Himmler orders all remaining ghettos to be emptied and their inhabitants killed

1944

23 March	Deportation of Jews from Greece (occupied by the Germans) begins
9 April	Two Jews escape from Auschwitz and send news of the camp out of **occupied** Europe to the **Allies**. News of the camp cannot now be ignored.
15 May	Mass deportation and gassing of Hungarian Jews begins
From June	Death marches from camps in the east, as prisoners are marched in front of advancing Soviet troops
6 June	Allied troops land in Normandy

1945

17 January	Final death march from Auschwitz-Birkenau
27 January	Soviet troops reach Auschwitz
11 April	US troops reach Buchenwald
15 April	British troops reach Belsen
29 April	US troops reach Dachau
30 April	Hitler commits suicide in Berlin, as the city is occupied by Soviet troops
5 May	US troops reach Mauthausen
7 May	Germany surrenders
20 November	Nuremberg trials of Nazi war criminals begin. First war criminals executed in October 1946.

Glossary

Allies used to mean the various countries that fought against Nazi Germany in the Second World War (1939–45)

anti-Semitism being prejudiced against Jewish people

Aryan used by the Nazis to mean people with northern European ancestors, without any ancestors from what they called 'inferior' races, such as Poles, Slavs or Jews. Aryans were supposed to be blonde, blue-eyed and sturdy.

camp *see* concentration camp, death camp, labour camp

concentration camp prison camp set up by the Nazis under a special law that meant that the prisoners were never tried and were never given a release date. The Nazis could put anyone in these camps, for any reason or none, for as long as they wanted.

crematoria places with special ovens for burning bodies

death camp camp set up by the Nazis to mass murder as many people, most of them Jewish people, as quickly and cheaply as possible. The SS who ran the death camps mostly gassed their victims.

displaced person (DP) camp camp set up after the war for 'displaced persons' – people who had been taken from their homes and countries and separated from their families. Workers in these camps tried to trace families and help a person to get back home.

Einsatzgruppen 'killing squad' sent into the Soviet Union with the invading army with the job of rounding up and killing as many Jewish people as possible. *Einsatzkommando 3* was a sub-unit of the *Einsatzgruppen*.

functionaries prisoners who worked as administrative officials for the Nazis

Gestapo secret police set up by the Nazis in 1933

ghetto area of a town or city, walled or fenced off from the rest of the city, where Jewish people were forced to live

guerrilla fighting small groups of people, fighting from hiding, using tactics like ambush; not open warfare

Holocaust in ancient times, the word 'Holocaust' meant 'an offering to the gods that was completely burnt away'. By medieval times it was used to mean 'a huge destruction or sacrifice'. From 1700 it was used to talk about the murder of large numbers of people. It is now mostly used to describe the deliberate attempt by the Nazi government in Germany to destroy all the Jewish people in their power.

Judenrat 'Jewish Council' – the people put in charge of the ghettos by the Nazis

kapo prisoner who was put in charge of other prisoners when they were working, making sure that they worked hard

Kindertransport name given to the British government's acceptance of about 10,000 Jewish children into Britain from Germany in 1939. These children had to have a home to go to, but they did not need visas, just proof of age and identity.

labour camp prison camp set up by the Nazis that used the prisoners as cheap labour

liberation used to mean a place, especially a camp, being freed from the control of the SS. Camps were liberated by Allied soldiers.

Nazi member of the Nazi party. It is short for *Nationalsozialistische Deutsche Arbeiterpartei*: the National Socialist German Workers' Party.

occupied the parts of Europe that the Nazis took over by force and then ran with Nazi officials, using the Gestapo and the army to keep people under control

papers used to mean all the different documents needed under Nazi rule – identity card, work permit, travel permit, Aryan certificate and so on

partisan someone who fights an army that has invaded and taken over their country

'political' person arrested for opposing Nazi ideas or actions

propaganda information and ideas given to people in a way that will make them accept these ideas

rabbi spiritual leader of a Jewish synagogue, who conducts the services and teaches and advises adults and children

race group of people with the same ancestors

racial inferiority Nazis' belief that some races were 'inferior', that is not as good as other races. They saw Jewish people as belonging to a separate race, one that was inferior to the German Aryan race.

Reich means 'empire'. *See* Third Reich.

resettlement to take people away from one place and make them settle somewhere else. Jewish people who were moved to the ghettos and then to the camps by the Nazis were promised they would be 'resettled' in the east.

resistance name given to groups formed in countries taken over by the Nazis to secretly fight the Nazis and try to drive them out of the country

roll call the count of all the prisoners in a camp, usually morning and evening

sabotage deliberately damaging something so it will not work

SS short for '*Schutzstaffel*' – security staff. The SS began as Hitler's personal guard. Later, they ran concentration camps and death camps. All the SS swore loyalty to Hitler, not Germany.

Third Reich means 'Third Empire'. The Nazis saw their rule as the third German empire, with Hitler as emperor.

transport used to refer to a trainload of people being sent to the camps

undesirable used by the Nazis to mean any person they disapproved of. People could be 'undesirable' because of their political beliefs, race, religion or behaviour.

Zionist person who believed in the setting up of a Jewish nation in Palestine

Further reading

Further reading

Auschwitz, Jane Shuter (Heinemann Library, 1999)

Diary of a Young Girl, Anne Frank (Penguin, 1997)

I Never Saw Another Butterfly, Hana Volavkova (Schocken Books, 1993)

Introducing the Holocaust, Haim Bresheeth, Stuart Hood and Litza Jansz (Icon Books, 2000)

Never to Forget: the Jews of the Holocaust, Milton Meltzer (*HarperCollins*, 1991)

Shadow of the Wall, Christa Laird (Red Fox, 1999)

The Hidden Children, Howard Greenfeld (Houghton Mifflin, 1997)

We Remember the Holocaust, David Adler (Henry Holt & Co, 1995)

Sources

The author and Publishers gratefully acknowledge the publications from which written sources in the book are drawn. In some cases the wording or sentence structure has been simplified to make the material appropriate for a school readership.

A Jump For Life, Ruth Altbeker Cyrus (Constable & Robinson Ltd, 1997) pp. 38–39

All But My Life, Gerda Weissmann Klein (Copyright © 1957, renewed 1995 by Gerda Weissmann Klein. Reprinted by permission of Hill and Wang, a division of Farrar, Straus and Giroux, LLC) pp. 7, 18–21

An Englishman in Auschwitz, Leon Greenman (Vallentine Mitchell, 2001) pp. 44–45

Auschwitz, A Doctor's Story, Lucie Adelsberger (Robson Books, 1997) pp. 30–31

Auschwitz Nazi Death Camp (Auschwitz-Birkenau State Museum, 1996) pp. 40–41

But I Survived, Tadeusz Sobolewicz (Auschwitz-Birkenau Memorial and Museum, Poland, 1998) pp. 7, 22–25

Chasing Shadows, Hugo Gryn (Viking, 2000) pp. 26–29

Kleins' website pp. 10–11

My Heart in a Suitcase, Anne L. Fox (Vallentine Mitchell, 1996) pp. 8–9

Never Again, Martin Gilbert (HarperCollins, 2000) pp. 40–41

Once There was a World, a 900 Year Chronicle of the Shtetl of Eishyshok, Yaffa Eliach (Little, Brown and Co, 1998) pp. 42–43

Playing For Time, Fania Fenelon (Syracuse University Press, 1977) pp. 32–35

The Avengers, Rich Cohen (Jonathan Cape, 2000) pp. 7, 16

The Hidden Children, Howard Greenfeld (Ticknor & Fields, 1993) pp. 12–15

The Journey Back From Hell, Anton Gill (HarperCollins, 1994) pp. 7, 36–37

Places of interest and websites

Museums and exhibitions

Imperial War Museum
Lambeth Road, London SE16 6HZ
Tel: 020 7416 5320
Website: *http://www.iwm.org.uk*
The Imperial War Museum in London now has a permanent Holocaust exhibition.

London Jewish Museum
Raymond Burton House, 129–131 Albert Street, London NW1 7NB
Tel: 020 7284 1997
Website: *http://www.jewishmuseum.org.uk*
Or:
The Sternberg Centre, 80 East End Road, London N3 2SY
Tel: 020 8349 1143
The two centres of the London Jewish Museum regularly feature exhibitions and talks about the Holocaust.

Sydney Jewish Museum
146 Darlinghurst Road, Darlinghurst, NSW 2010, Australia
Tel: (02) 9360 7999
Website: *www.join.org.au/sydjmus/*
The Sydney Jewish Museum contains a permanent Holocaust exhibition, using survivors of the Holocaust as guides.

Websites

Before consulting any websites you need to know:

1 Almost all Holocaust websites have been designed for adult users. They can contain horrifying and upsetting information and pictures.
2 Some people wish to minimize the Holocaust, or even deny that it happened at all. Some of their websites pretend to be delivering unbiased facts and information. To be sure of getting accurate information it is always better to use an officially recognized site such as the ones listed below.

www.ushmm.org
This is the US Holocaust Memorial Museum site.

www.iwm.org.uk
The Imperial War Museum site. You can access Holocaust material from the main page.

www.holocaust-history.org
This is the Holocaust History Project site.

www.auschwitz.dk
The Holocaust: Crimes, Heroes and Villains site.

http://motlc.wiesenthal.com
The Museum of Tolerance's Multimedia Learning Centre site.

Index